EVERY KID'S GUIDE TO
SAVING THE EARTH
BY JOY BERRY

Ideals Children's Books • Nashville, Tennessee

Managing Editor: Cathy Vertuca
Copy Editor: Annette Gooch
Editorial Assistant: Wendy Nicholson

Art Direction: Communication Graphics
Design: Jack and Donna Fisher
Illustration Design: Bartholomew
Inking and Coloring: Bernice Happé Iriks
Composition and Production: Toni Douglass

Published by Forest House Publishing Co., Inc.
in cooperation with Living Skills Press

Trade paperback edition published by
Ideals Publishing Corporation
Nashville, Tennessee 37214

ISBN 0-8249-8554-0 (paperback)

1 2 3 4 5 6 7 8 9 R 00 99 98 97 96 95 94 93

TABLE OF CONTENTS

All human beings need energy to survive and grow.
Energy comes from natural resources, such as air, gas, water, and coal,
found in and around the earth.

The earth has a limited supply of natural resources.
If they are used carelessly, there will not be enough for human beings to use.

For this reason, it is important not to waste natural resources.

It is important to do all you can to help conserve the earth's natural resources.
When you do this, you are contributing to your own survival and growth,
as well as to that of other living beings.

It is important to avoid wasting water.
Be careful how you use it.
You can conserve water by doing these things:

Do not allow water to run from a faucet unless you are using it.

☐

At the bathroom sink, do not allow water to run while you are brushing your teeth. Instead, wet your toothbrush and then turn off the water until you are ready to rinse your mouth.

☐

In the shower, turn off the water while you soap your body and shampoo your hair. Turn it on again when you are ready to rinse.

When you let the kitchen tap run to get hot water,

☐

use the cool water for the garbage disposal, or

☐

collect the cool water in a pitcher and use it for drinking water, watering plants, or filling the washing machine.

When you let the shower run to get hot water, do not allow the water to run any longer than necessary.

☐

Do not let the shower run while you undress and prepare for your shower.

Do not use more water than you need.

If you fill the tub half full, you will have more than enough water to take a bath.

Only flush the toilet to dispose of body wastes. Dispose of used materials such as facial tissues in a wastebasket instead of the toilet.

Use hot water only when you actually need it.

Use water from the cold-water faucet whenever possible. This saves hot water and energy by preventing the water heater from turning on.

Remind the adults in your home that the temperature gauge on the water heater should be set at approximately 140° or lower to save energy.

Remind the adults in your home that an insulated cover for the water heater would help keep the water hot and would save energy and money.

You will use less water with every flush if you place this
TOILET WATER SAVER
in the water tank of your toilet.

Leaving lights on in rooms that are not being used wastes energy.
Therefore, it is important to turn off lights when they are not needed.

Turning a light on and off too much can shorten the life of the light bulb.

You should turn off a regular (incandescent) light
if you are going to leave the room for more than 3 minutes at a time.

You should turn off a fluorescent light
if you are going to leave the room for more than 15 minutes at a time.

Electricity is needed to turn on light bulbs.
Electricity is a valuable resource that needs to be used sparingly.
How many light bulbs can you find in this picture?

For your comfort and safety,
the temperature in your home should be
approximately 68°F in the winter and 78°F in the summer.

Heaters and air conditioners use a lot of energy, so people should not depend on these appliances alone to maintain the proper temperature in their homes. Here are energy-saving ways to keep a home warm in the winter and cool in the summer.

Make sure that all the openings such as windows or doors are closed
when you are heating or cooling your home.
This helps keep the heated or cooled air from escaping.

☐
Keep doors and
windows closed when
the heater or air
conditioner is on.

☐
Close the damper when
the fireplace is not in
use. Hot ashes should
be allowed to cool
before you do this.

It is a good idea to keep the drapes and window shades closed on cold days to keep the cold air outside.

If you still feel cold when the room temperature is 68°F or more, wear warmer clothing like a sweater or jacket, or do something active to warm your body.

WOW...MAN I'M STILL FREEZING.

SITTING IS **NOT** ACTIVE.

TOO BAD YOU DON'T HAVE A FUR COAT.

On cold nights, keep warm by using extra blankets and wearing heavier nightclothes.

HUMPH! I'M CHILLY. BETTER CRANK UP THE OLD HEAT.

SNUGGLING FURRY PETS HELPS TOO!

Keep the drapes and shades closed
on hot summer days too. This will conserve resources
by keeping out the hot rays of the sun!

If you still feel warm
when the room
temperature is 78°F
or less,

☐

wear lightweight
clothing,

☐
do something less
active to reduce your
body heat,
☐
wipe a damp, cool cloth
over your skin, or
☐
place a damp, cool cloth
on your forehead or on
the back of your neck.

On hot nights, keep
cool by wearing
lightweight nightclothes,
and using only a sheet
or light blanket to cover
yourself.

Can you find the 5 things these people are doing
to conserve heat?

It takes energy to run appliances.
The less you use an appliance, the more energy you save.
If you can do a task without using an appliance, do it.

Here are some ways
to save energy:

☐

Wash and dry dishes by
hand instead of using a
dishwasher.

☐

Dry your hair with a
towel instead of using a
hair dryer.

THAT'S IT!
GIVE THOSE
APPLIANCES
A REST.

☐

Wash small loads of
laundry by hand instead
of using a washing
machine.

☐

Hang laundry up to dry
instead of using a
clothes dryer.

I CAN WASH THESE
THREE PAIRS OF
SOCKS JUST AS
EASILY BY HAND.

WHAT A
BRIGHT
IDEA.

GUESS WHOSE ROOM THIS IS?

Do not leave appliances on when no one is using them.

THIS IS NOTHING TO CLOWN AROUND WITH...

BOO
ROCK-A
ROCK-A
DOO
DOO
DO-WA
DO-WA

☐
Do not leave the TV on when no one is watching it.

☐
Do not leave a radio on when no one is listening to it.

AND NOW HERE'S...

CLiCK

SNORE
ZZZ

SKiTCH
SKiTCH
SKiTCH

☐
Do not leave audio equipment on when the record, tape, or CD has finished playing.

WHAT A GREAT WORK-OUT! OFF TO THE SHOWER!

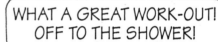

OFF

SSSSSSs

☐
Do not leave electric irons, tools, or toys plugged in when no one is using them.

☐
Do not leave curling irons, steam curlers, or hair dryers plugged in when no one is using them. Since electric appliances can be dangerous, ask an adult to help you.

POCK

Because large appliances use more energy than small ones,
use small appliances instead of larger ones whenever you have a choice.

The energy supply is limited during the daytime,
when large appliances in homes and businesses get the most use.
Whenever you have a choice, use large appliances
early in the morning or late at night, when more energy is available.

RIBBIT...

THAT'S FROG TALK FOR TOTALLY LAME.

Here are some ways to save resources when doing laundry:

OH OH YEAH!

I JUST NEED A FEW THINGS WASHED...

OH WELL...

☐ Wash only full loads whenever you use the washing machine. If you do not have enough laundry for a full load, adjust the water level for smaller loads. Do not use more water than is necessary.

☐ Use the short cycle on the washing machine whenever possible.

I'D SAY THAT QUALIFIES AS A FULL LOAD.

I ONLY NEEDED MY TENNIS SHOES DRIED.

THUD THUMP

☐ Do not use the dryer to dry only one or two articles. Instead, hang up the items to dry.

☐ Do not overload the dryer. A very large load takes longer to dry than several smaller loads.

WATCH THAT SPIN CYCLE...

HUMPH...I FORGOT TO SHUT OFF THE DRYER.

YEAH, IT'S ONLY BEEN RUNNING AN HOUR.

☐ Turn off the dryer as soon as the laundry is dry. Do not waste energy by allowing the dryer to run longer than necessary.

☐ Keeping the lint screen clean makes the dryer work more efficiently, so laundry dries faster. Therefore, clean the lint from the screen each time you use the dryer.

LINT MAKES A GOOD NEST FOR MICE!

Here are some ways to use kitchen appliances effectively:

When the refrigerator or freezer door is left open, warm air from the room raises the temperature inside the appliance. Lowering the temperature enough to keep the food cold requires extra energy. You can save energy by doing these things:

□ Decide what you need from the refrigerator or freezer before you open the door.
□ Open and close the door as quickly as possible.
□ Make sure that the door is not left ajar when you close it.

I CAN'T DECIDE.

HMMM...

SHUT

HOW ABOUT SOME ANCHOVIES?

□ Heating a small pan on a large burner wastes energy. Therefore, use pans that match the size of the stove burners you are using. Since cooking can be dangerous, ask an adult to help you.

FISH STEW?

□ Run the dishwasher only when it contains a full load.
□ Use the short cycle of the dishwasher whenever possible.
□ Turn off the dishwasher after the last rinse cycle. Open the door slightly, leave it ajar, and allow the dishes to air-dry.

COME ON, COME ON, I NEED A CLEAN GLASS.

UH-HUH!

Here are some other ways to save resources when you use appliances:

During an electrical storm, unplug the television set and all other small appliances to protect them from possible damage.

Remind an adult to turn down the thermostats on the water heater, refrigerator, and freezer in your home.

How many appliances in this picture
can be turned off before the family leaves
on a long trip away from home?

Do not allow water to run unattended.
Turn the water off as soon as you have finished using it.
You can conserve water outdoors by doing these things:

☐ When you water the garden or lawn, watch to see that the plants receive enough water and then turn the water off.

☐ If you cannot be present while the yard is being watered, set a time limit for the watering and return to turn the water off when the time is up.

☐ When you water a garden or lawn during the heat of the day, much of the water is lost through evaporation. Therefore, water the yard during the early morning or in the evening.

☐ Eliminate weeds so that they don't use water needed by the plants growing in your lawn and garden.

Help save gasoline by using a car for transportation only when it is necessary.
You can help save gasoline by using
these forms of transportation whenever possible:

□
walk,
□
ride a bike,
□
use public
transportation such as
buses or trains, or
□
share rides with
your friends.

Cars run more
efficiently and thus use
less energy when their
windows are closed.
Therefore, you should
keep car windows
rolled up whenever
possible. Also, car
heaters and air
conditioners should be
used as little as possible.

Walking or riding a bike saves gasoline.
Use your finger to trace the pedestrian's path from
home to the store.

One way to save energy is to use things for as long as possible
so that more of the same products do not need to be produced.
To get the most use out of items, do these things:

☐ Take care of the things you use and store them carefully when you are finished with them.

☐ Repair things when they become worn or broken.

☐ Use rechargeable batteries rather than the throw-away kind.

☐ Use an entire sheet of paper (including both sides) before discarding it.

☐ Clean and reuse glass or plastic items whenever possible.

Recycling helps save natural resources and energy by putting things to new uses.
To help save energy and other resources, recycle items instead of throwing them away.
Many different things can be recycled.

Save used newspaper, glass, and cans and take them to recycling centers
so that they can be made into new products.

You can make your own
RECYCLING RECEPTACLE.
Here's how:

☐
Find 3 cardboard boxes
of the same size and
line them up in a row.
☐
Punch 2 holes in the
right side of the first
box and in the left side
of the middle box.

OOPS! WRONG
PUNCH!

☐
Put heavy string
through the holes and
tie the two boxes
together.
☐
Punch 2 holes in the
right side of the middle
box and in the left side
of the third box.

□
Label the first box *glass*, the middle box *aluminum*, and the third box *metal* (non-aluminum).

□
Thread heavy string through the holes and tie the three boxes together.

□
Set an open paper bag (made from recycled paper) in each box to hold the recyclable items.

□
When the bags are filled, take them to a recycling center.

□
Put empty open bags in the three boxes and start filling them again.

Note: You might want to set a fourth box by your recycling receptacle to hold old newspapers or plastic items.

CONSERVING RESOURCES IN OTHER WAYS – RECYCLING

You need to properly prepare materials before you take them to a recycling center.

Be sure all materials are clean.
Then separate them into the following categories:

☐
Glass
☐
Aluminum
(Aluminum cans are
light and have no
seams; magnets do not
stick to them.)

☐
Metal (non-aluminum)
(These cans are heavier
than aluminum cans
and have seams;
magnets stick to them.)
☐
Newspaper

How to prepare materials
for recycling:

□ To prepare glass containers, remove all aluminum caps and rings, and put these with the aluminum items. Remove all metal lids and put these with the metal items. Remove all labels.

□ To prepare aluminum cans, remove the paper labels and the lids. Then flatten the cans and put them with the TV dinner trays, cake tins, and foil.

□ To prepare metal cans, remove the paper labels and the tops and bottoms from the cans.

□ To prepare newspapers, stack and tie them together with string. Do not include magazines or other printed materials that use "coated stock" paper.

SOAK THE LABEL TO MAKE IT EASY TO REMOVE.

BE CAREFUL WITH SHARP EDGES!

I'M WATCHING OUT FOR THOSE SHARP EDGES!

HEY, WAIT! I'M STILL READING!

Recycle grass clippings, leaves, and food scraps by composting them.
Compost is a kind of fertilizer. It consists of decomposed organic material
that can be used to enrich the soil in lawns and gardens.

You can make your own
COMPOSTING BIN.
Here's how:

□
Get 3 to 4 yards of wire fencing (enough to make a compost bin approximately 3 feet across and 3 feet tall).

□
Form the fencing into a circle.

□
Fasten the two ends of the fencing together with wire to form the bin.

YOU COULD EVEN USE CHICKEN WIRE.

□
Place the composting bin in a shaded area so the compost will stay moist enough to decompose properly.

□
Make a lid of screen to keep out the flies.

□
Turn the contents in the bin about once a week to keep the compost well mixed.

DRAT!

Here's how to make
COMPOST IN A GARBAGE BAG.

In a large, heavy-duty polyethylene garbage bag, alternate layers of the following:
4 inches of cuttings, leaves, and shrub trimmings,
a sprinkling of water, and
garden soil.

☐ Continue layering until the bag is filled. Cover the compost with sawdust to reduce fly problems.

☐ Lightly water the compost as needed to keep it moist but not soggy.

☐ Turn the contents in the bag about once a week to keep the compost well-mixed.

MISCELLANEOUS NOTES ABOUT COMPOST

☐ If the compost begins to smell like ammonia or rotten eggs, cover the top layer of the compost with approximately 1 inch of sawdust and turn the compost daily.

☐ Add food scraps as long as they do not include meat scraps, bones, or fat.

☐ Compost mixed with soil makes a good potting mixture for plants or seeds.

You can make your own
RECYCLED PAPER.
Since blenders can be dangerous, ask an adult to help you with this project.

☐ Place a 9- by 12-inch piece of window screen in a 10- by 15-inch baking sheet with sides.

☐ Tear up used paper into small pieces.

☐ Fill a blender container halfway with water.

☐ Turn on the blender and add the paper pieces to the water, blending until the mixture has a thick, mud-like consistency.

☐ Spread the mixture evenly onto the screen.

All human beings need fresh air to breathe and pure water to drink.
They also survive and grow better in an environment that is peaceful, clean, and beautiful.

To make sure these essentials are available, it is important that human beings avoid polluting their environment. Humans pollute their environment when they do things to damage the natural state of air, water, and other resources.

STOPPING POLLUTION

Pollutants are substances that, when released into the environment,
are harmful rather than helpful.

It is important to do all you can to avoid polluting the earth and its surroundings.
When you do this, you contribute to your own survival and
growth, as well as to that of all living things.

STOPPING AIR POLLUTION – TOXIC PRODUCTS

Some products damage the ozone layer
(a protective layer in the earth's atmosphere) and create pollution.
These products are toxic (harmful) and you should avoid using them whenever possible.

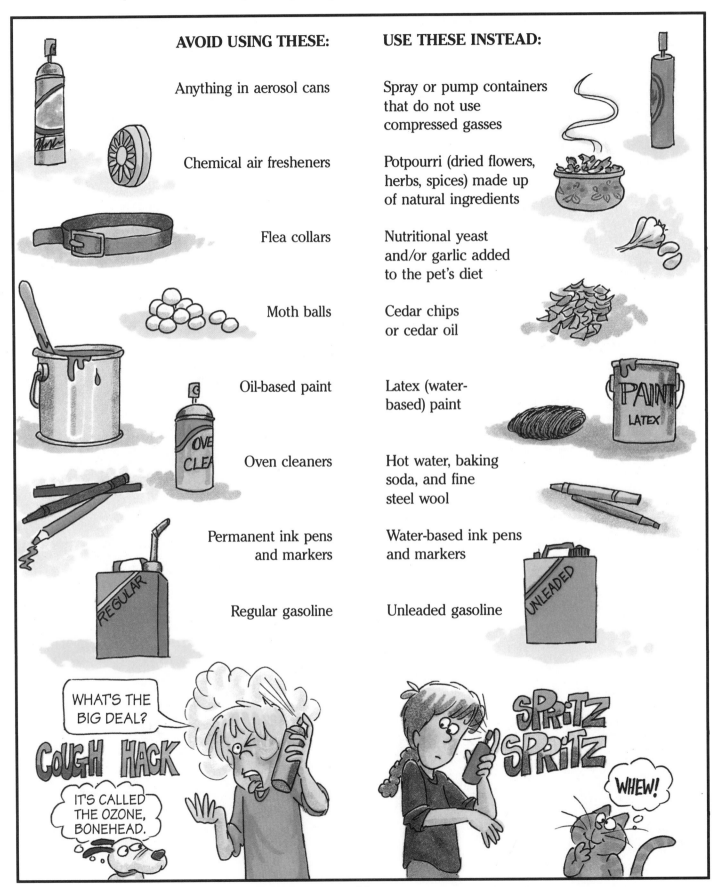

AVOID USING THESE:

Anything in aerosol cans

Chemical air fresheners

Flea collars

Moth balls

Oil-based paint

Oven cleaners

Permanent ink pens and markers

Regular gasoline

USE THESE INSTEAD:

Spray or pump containers that do not use compressed gasses

Potpourri (dried flowers, herbs, spices) made up of natural ingredients

Nutritional yeast and/or garlic added to the pet's diet

Cedar chips or cedar oil

Latex (water-based) paint

Hot water, baking soda, and fine steel wool

Water-based ink pens and markers

Unleaded gasoline

WHAT'S THE BIG DEAL?

COUGH HACK

IT'S CALLED THE OZONE, BONEHEAD.

SPRITZ SPRITZ

WHEW!

The smoke and residue from fires can pollute the air.
Therefore, people need to be careful when they burn things.
Since fires can be dangerous, ask an adult to help you.

□ Trash should not be burned. Instead, it should be taken or sent to a public dump, where it can be buried or burned safely.

□ Nothing should be burned in fireplaces other than wood or wood substitutes that are environmentally safe.

SO, BURNING THOSE PLASTIC BOTTLES ISN'T A GOOD IDEA.

THIS SOUNDS LIKE IT'LL BE FUN.

Trees take in carbon dioxide and give off oxygen.
Planting trees can help purify the air.

HOW TO GROW A TREE:

You can grow trees from acorns, chestnuts, and many other kinds of seeds produced by trees in autumn.

☐ Plant a seed in a pot and water it.

BE CAREFUL NOT TO OVERWATER.

☐ Put a plastic bag over the pot to keep the soil damp. Then put the pot in a sunny place.

PLENTY OF SUNSHINE.

☐ Remove the plastic bag in approximately 2 months when a seedling appears. Then water it every week.

The best time to plant a tree
is in the autumn.

(Ask an adult to help you with this project.)

☐
Plant the seedling
outside when it is too
big for the pot. Place
the seedling in a hole
that is a bit bigger
than the pot.

☐
Fill in the hole with soil
and press it down.

☐
Drive a strong stick into
the ground next to the
seedling and tie the
seedling to it. Then
water the young tree
as often as
necessary.

Hazardous wastes can ruin the water supply needed to keep plants, animals, and humans alive and healthy. Hazardous wastes should never be disposed of in a sink, all drains (like tubs, etc.), or a toilet. They should never be dumped on the ground or into gutters.

Hazardous wastes need to be kept in their original containers and clearly labeled. They need to be stored in cool, dry places where children cannot get to them.

Hazardous wastes need to be recycled by a licensed contractor or recycling agency or to be destroyed at a public incinerator.

Soaps and detergents can pollute the water supply.
You can help protect the water supply from pollution
by doing these things:

☐ Use as little soap as possible to wash yourself.

☐ Use as little shampoo as possible to wash your hair.

☐ Use as little detergent (and other laundry products) as possible to do your laundry.

☐ Use low-phosphate or phosphate-free detergent for laundry and dishes, if possible.

There are many hazardous wastes and water pollutants
in these pictures.

How many can you find?

Trash not only spoils the natural beauty
of the environment,
it pollutes the environment as well.

☐ Dispose of all your trash in a trash receptacle.

☐ Pick up any trash you come across and put it in a trash receptacle.

☐ Take trash bags with you on outings. Store your trash in them until you can dispose of it in a trash receptacle.

☐ Keep a trash bag in your car. Put your trash in it while you are traveling in the car. Then empty the bag when you return home.

Trash accumulating on the earth spoils the beauty of the environment and also takes up valuable room that could be living space for plants, animals, and humans.

HE'S A WALKING ENVIRONMENTAL HAZARD!

It is important to limit the amount of trash you create. You can limit the amount of trash you contribute to the environment by doing these things:

☐ Whenever possible, avoid buying plastic and other products that do not decompose.

THE PICNIC WILL BE FUN!

I WONDER WHERE THOSE ARE GOING TO END UP?

WEEEE

☐ Do not release helium balloons into the atmosphere. They eventually fall back to earth as litter and do not decompose.

TIE TIE

UM...GIMME A BAG.

☐ Do not accept a shopping bag for purchases that you can carry without a bag.

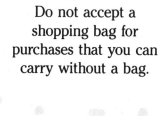

...NO THANKS, I CAN CARRY THESE.

STOPPING ENVIRONMENTAL POLLUTION – CLUTTER

Because clutter spoils the beauty of the environment,
it is important to keep the areas you occupy clean and organized.
This includes your bedroom and areas where you work and play.

Find the areas in this house that need to be cleaned and organized.

Disposable items are designed to be used once and then thrown away. Although disposable items are convenient, they don't disappear after being discarded. They must be burned in incinerators or buried in garbage dumps and landfills. These processes use energy and contribute to air and land pollution.

For these reasons, you should avoid using disposable items when possible. For example, use cloth towels and napkins instead of paper ones. Use plates that can be washed and reused instead of disposable ones. Buy beverages in returnable containers instead of disposable ones.

If you must use disposable items, use them sparingly. For example, do not waste toilet paper and facial tissue.

Loud noises can destroy the serenity of the environment.
You can help reduce noise pollution
by doing these things:

☐
Keep your voice at a normal (acceptable) level when you are around other people.

☐
If you need or want to do anything that makes noise (such as playing a musical instrument), do it when and where the noise will not disturb others.

☐
Keep the volume on the TV, radio, and tape player at a level that will not bother others.

You can use a large, cardboard appliance box to
MAKE A PLACE
where you can find peace and quiet or make noise. (Ask an adult to help you with this project.)

☐ Turn the box upside down.

☐ Make a hinged door by cutting two vertical lines that are approximately 2 feet long and 1 foot apart.

☐ Fold up the flap created by the two cuts at the bottom edge of the box. Make hinged windows by making two vertical cuts approximately 1 foot long and approximately 1 foot apart.

☐ Connect the two vertical cuts at the bottom with one horizontal cut.

☐ Fold up the door or window flaps you have created.

☐ Take a flashlight and whatever else you plan to use into your special place.

NOW ALL WE NEED ARE SOME FISH STICKS!

Animals and plants are an important part of the environment. It is important to help them survive by preserving the places where they live.

One of the greatest threats to animals and plants is a forest fire. Be extremely careful when you use matches or fire outdoors. Douse all fires and burning materials with water or cover them with dirt to make sure they will not continue to burn after you are finished using them.

HOW TO BUILD A SAFE CAMPFIRE: (Ask an adult to help you with this project.)

□ Clear an area of ground approximately 3 feet by 3 feet.
□ Dig a hole in the middle.
□ Place rocks around the rim of the hole.

□ Place kindling and wood inside the hole.
□ Ignite the kindling.
□ Do not leave the campfire unattended.

Remember to leave the campsite the way it looked before you came.

To preserve the places where animals live,
it is important not to disturb or move their homes.

You can create new homes for birds by recycling used containers.
Here are a few ideas for what you can do:

To preserve animal life, it is important not to do anything
that could poison or destroy their water or food supply.

You can improve the food supply for animals whose food supplies are threatened
by making the following foods available in their environment:

☐
Birds

Wild bird food, chicken feed, seeds, nuts, dried and fresh fruits, peanut butter, bread or cracker crumbs, uncooked grains and cereal, dog food, and suet (animal fat)

☐
Chipmunks

Hamster food, whole-grain bread, uncooked grains, and sunflower seeds

☐
Deer

Edible seed shrubs

☐
Hummingbirds

A solution consisting of 1 tablespoon of sugar, 2 tablespoons of water, and several drops of red food coloring

☐
Opossums

Canned dog food and raw eggs

☐
Raccoons

Canned dog food and raw eggs

☐
Squirrels

Hamster food, whole-grain bread, uncooked grains, and sunflower seeds

You can create
FOOD HOLDERS FOR ANIMALS
by recycling used containers and objects.
Here are a few ideas for what you can do:

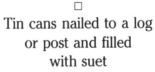

☐ Jar (containing hummingbird solution) turned upside down on a pie pan

☐ Plastic berry basket wired to a large plastic lid and filled with sunflower seeds

☐ Twine attached to each corner of the bottom of a cardboard box

☐ Tin cans nailed to a log or post and filled with suet

☐ Mesh bag filled with suet

☐ Pinecone holding suet and/or peanut butter with seeds

PRESERVING PLANTS – GROWING PLANTS

One of the best ways to help preserve nature is to grow plants.

You can start plants from seeds, seedlings, bulbs, roots, or cuttings. You can learn how to grow plants by reading books from your local library or by talking to people at your local nursery.

The plants you grow can provide beautiful flowers to enjoy, good food to eat, and herbs to enhance your cooking and health.

Here are two **PLANTS YOU CAN GROW** without a lot of effort or supplies:

AVOCADO PLANT
☐
Use an avocado seed,
4 toothpicks stuck into the seed to hold it
half in water and half out, and
a jar filled with water.

SWEET POTATO PLANT
☐
Use a sweet potato,
4 toothpicks stuck into the potato to hold it
half in water and half out, and
a jar filled with water.

Most plants need healthy soil in which to grow.

Earthworms help create healthy soil by contributing calcium to it, improving its texture, and helping water and air reach plant roots.

You can start an **EARTHWORM FARM.** The earthworms you raise can be placed in the lawn or garden. They can also serve as food for birds and other animals. The soil from your earthworm farm will make excellent compost for vegetable gardening.

☐ Fill a large pan or wooden box ⅔ full with a mixture of moist soil and leaves.

☐ Add a few earthworms to the mixture.

☐ Cover the box with plastic or a burlap cloth.

☐ Place the farm in a cool, but not freezing, location, such as a shady corner of the garden.

☐ Feed the worms kitchen leftovers, leaves, or manure.

SAVE THE EARTH PERSONAL SURVEY

YES NO

☐ ☐ I conserve water by turning faucets completely off when I am finished using them.

☐ ☐ I turn off lamps and other lights in rooms that are not being used.

☐ ☐ I conserve energy where possible in keeping our home warm in the winter and cool in the summer.

☐ ☐ I make sure that I turn off appliances as soon as I have finished using them.

☐ ☐ When watering the lawn, I am careful not to let the hose or sprinkler run unattended.

☐ ☐ To help conserve gasoline, I walk, ride my bike, use public transportation, or share rides with friends when possible.

☐ ☐ I get the greatest possible use from items by always using and storing them carefully.

☐ ☐ I recycle my outgrown clothes and unwanted toys by giving them to others who can use them.

☐ ☐ Whenever possible, I choose products that are not toxic.

☐ ☐ I am careful never to burn anything in a fireplace other than wood or wood products.

YES NO

☐ ☐ Whenever possible, I help purify the air by planting and growing trees.

☐ ☐ I am careful when handling and disposing of hazardous wastes such as paint and paint thinner.

☐ ☐ When I bathe or shower, I use only as much soap as necessary to get myself clean.

☐ ☐ When I go on an outing, I take along a trash bag and dispose of all my litter in a trash receptacle.

☐ ☐ I keep my room clean, well-organized, and free of clutter.

☐ ☐ When possible, I choose beverages in returnable containers instead of disposable ones.

☐ ☐ I do all I can to reduce noise pollution by keeping the volume as low as possible on the TV, radio, and other audio equipment.

☐ ☐ When I am outdoors, I am careful to avoid doing anything that could destroy places where animals live.

☐ ☐ I am careful to avoid harming the water or food supply of animals.

☐ ☐ Whenever possible, I help preserve nature by growing plants.

If you can say "yes" to most of these items, congratulations and thank you, because you are doing your part to *Save the Earth!*